Stinker does not

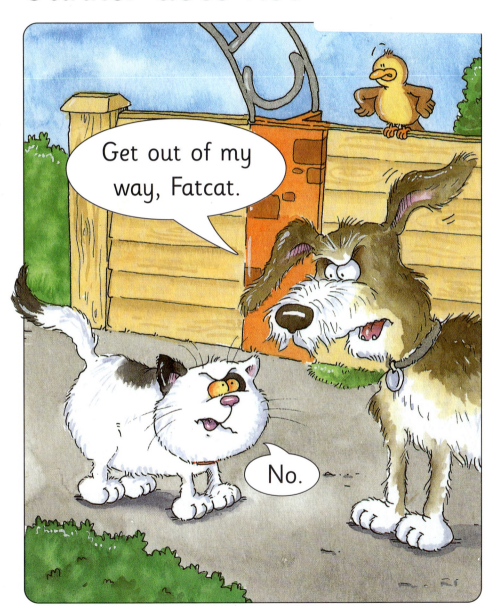

Fatcat does not like dogs.

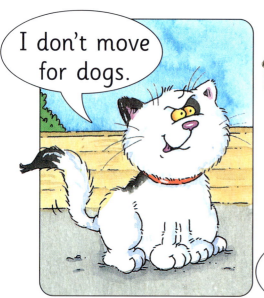

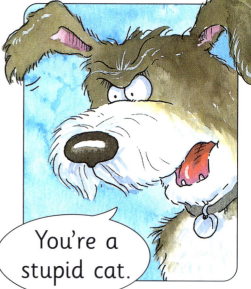

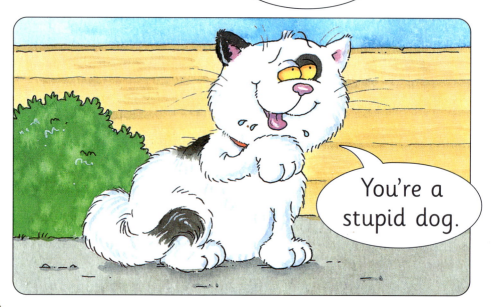

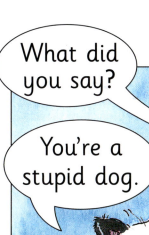

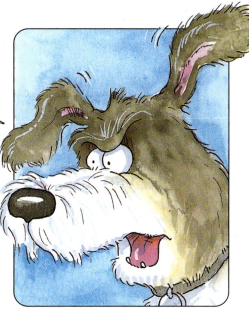

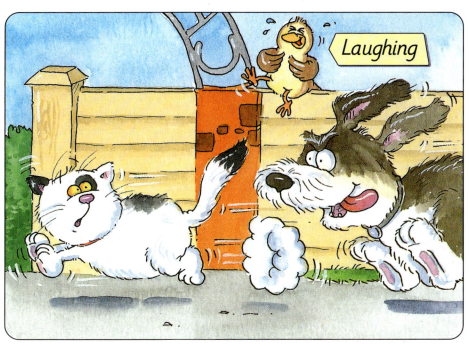

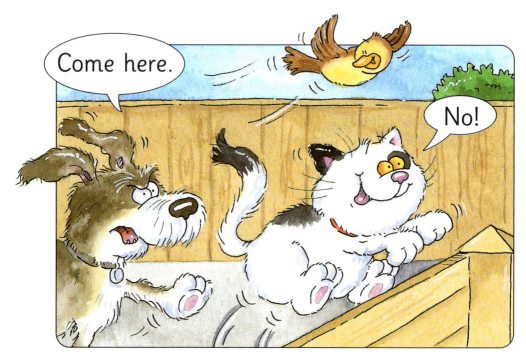

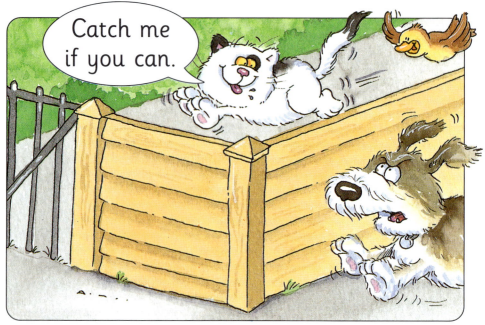

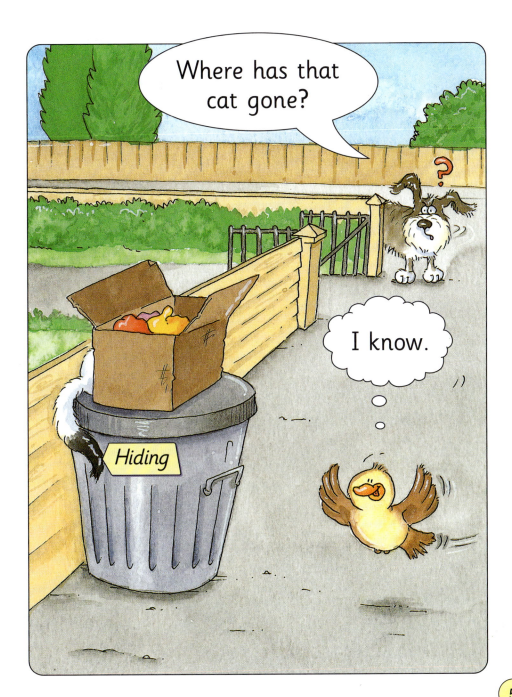

5

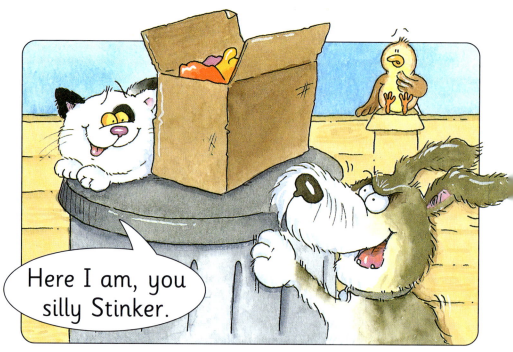

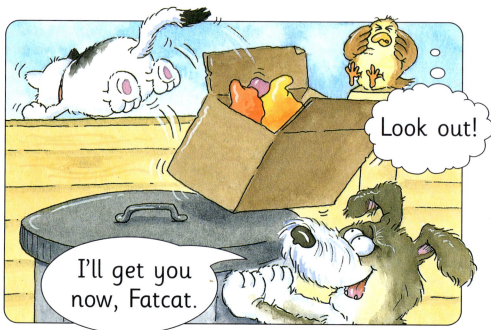

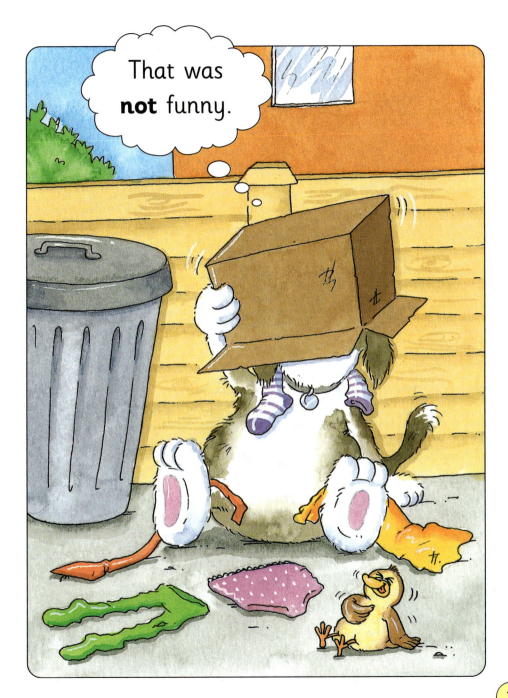

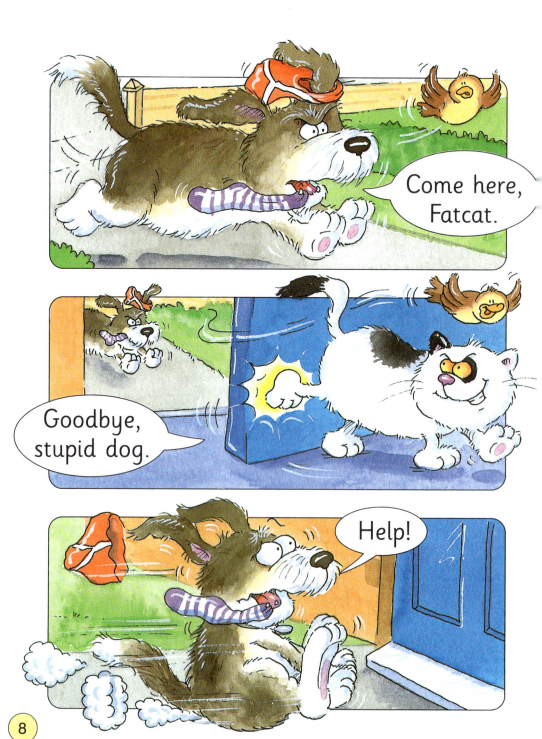

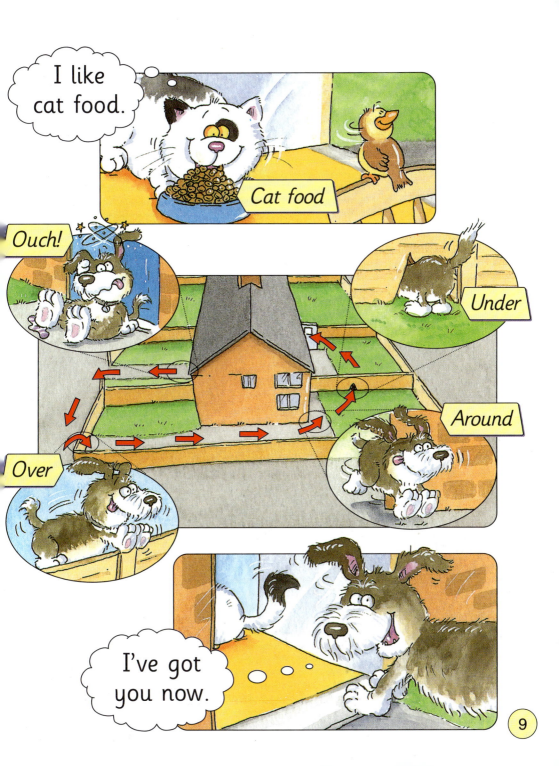

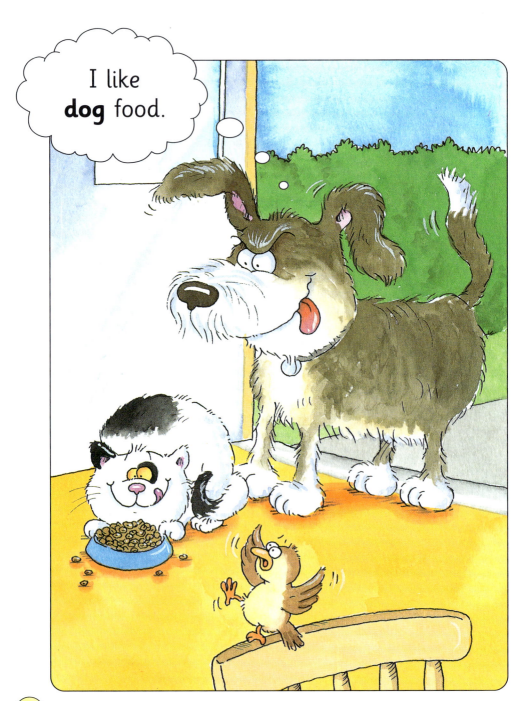

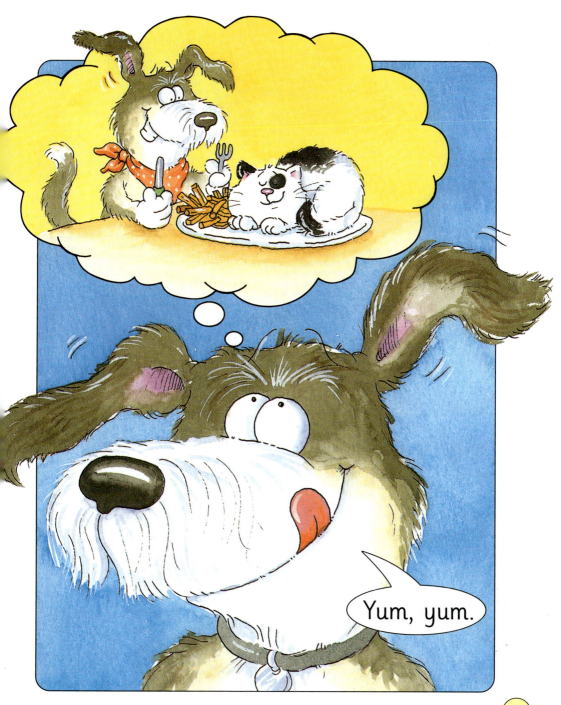

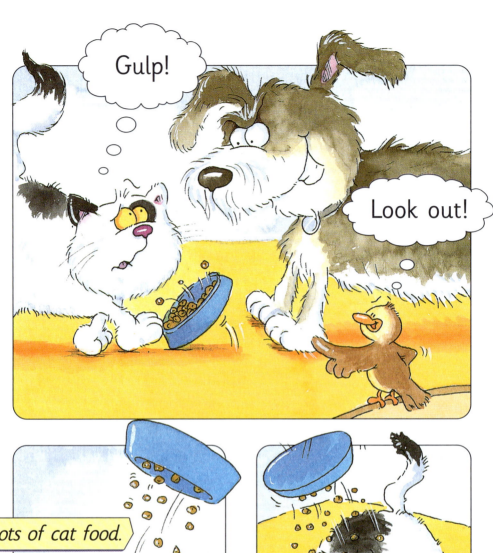

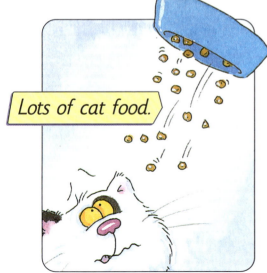

Lots of cat food.

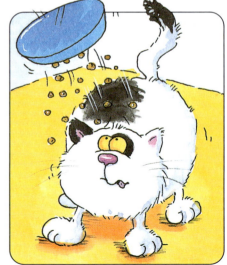

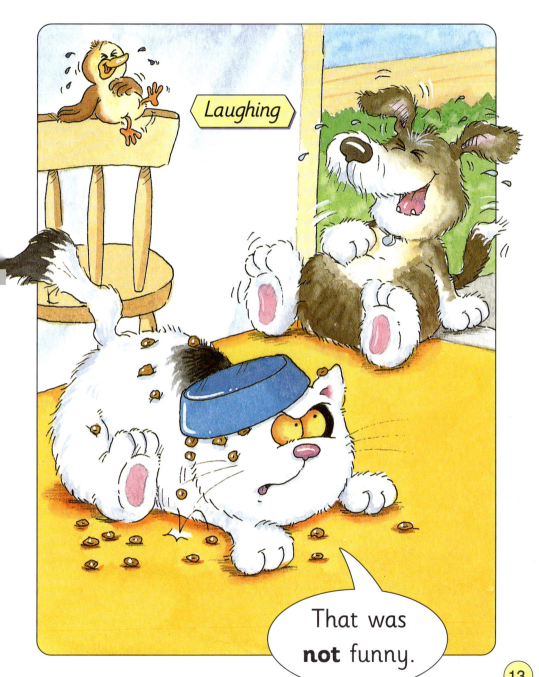

13

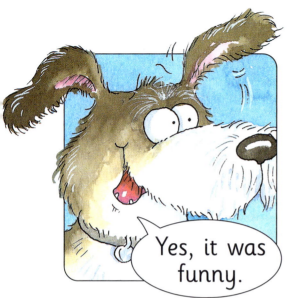

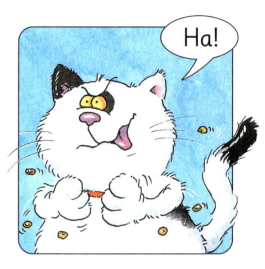

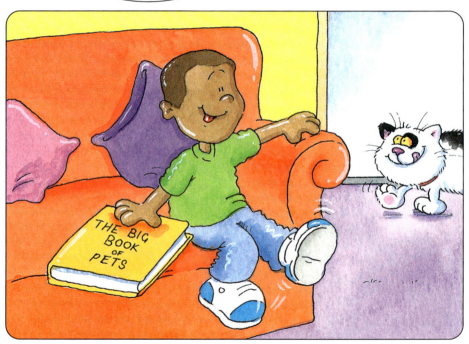

Ben calls Fatcat.

Ben likes cats.

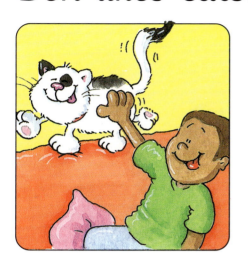 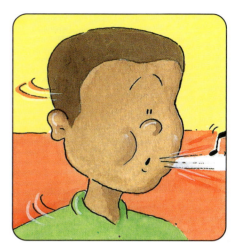

Ben calls Stinker.

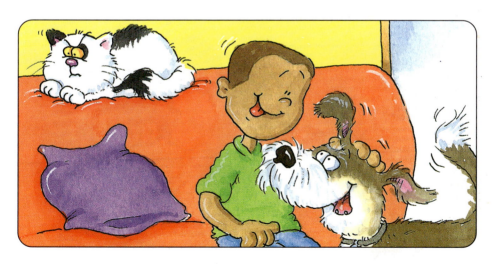

Ben likes dogs.

Fatcat and Stinker like Ben ...

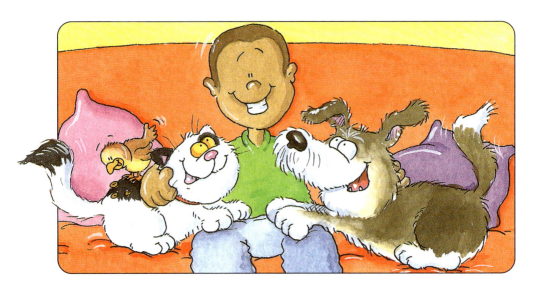

... but not each other.

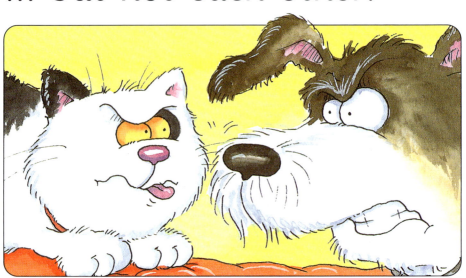